Belair Early Years I.C.T.

info

Graham Parton

Acknowledgements

The author and publisher would like to thank the staff and children of Kent College Infant and Junior School and Chartham County Primary School for their much appreciated contributions of work and artwork during the writing of this book.

The author would also like to thank his wife and family for their support during the writing and preparation of this book.

Published by Collins, An imprint of HarperCollins*Publishers*
77 – 85 Fulham Palace Road, Hammersmith, London, W6 8JB

Browse the complete Collins catalogue at
www.collinseducation.com

© HarperCollins*Publishers* Limited 2012
Previously published in 2007 by Folens
First published in 2000 by Belair Publications

10 9 8 7 6 5 4 3 2 1

ISBN-13 978-0-00-744794-7

Graham Parton asserts his moral rights to be identified as the author of this work

British Library Cataloguing in Publication Data
A Catalogue record for this publication is available from the British Library

All Early learning goals, Areas of learning and development, and Aspects of learning quoted in this book are taken from the *Statutory Framework for the Early Years Foundation Stage*, Department for Education, 2012 (available at www.education.gov.uk/publications). This information is licensed under the terms of the Open Government Licence (www.nationalarchives.gov.uk/doc/open-government-licence).

Every effort has been made to trace copyright holders and to obtain their permission for the use of copyright material. The authors and publishers will gladly receive any information enabling them to rectify any error or omission in subsequent editions.

Cover concept: Mount Deluxe   Cover design: Linda Miles, Lodestone Publishing
Cover photography: Nigel Meager   Editor: Elizabeth Miles
Page layout: Jane Conway   Photography: Roger Brown, Steve Forrest and Kelvin Freeman

DinoDon used by permission of aol.com; *Dazzle* used by permission of Silica Software Systems and Granada Learning Ltd.; *Cambridge Talking Books* used by permission of Sherston Software; *Textease* used by permission of Softease Limited.; Screen shots from *My World for Windows*, by Semerc Software, courtesy of Granada Learning Ltd.; Screen shots from *Yahoo!* courtesy of Yahoo! Inc.; Screen shots from *Counting Pictures* courtesy of BlackCat, a division of Granada Learning Ltd.; *Superlogo* courtesy of Longman Logotron Ltd.
Photographs: p.7 ©Terrie.L.Zeller/Shutterstock.com; p.9 ©Morgan Lane Photography/Shutterstock.com; p.10 ©Monkey Business Images/Shutterstock.com; p.11 ©Agan/Shutterstock.com

Printed and bound by Printing Express Limited, Hong Kong

MIX
Paper from responsible sources
FSC www.fsc.org   FSC C007454

Contents

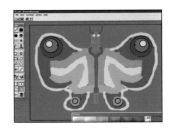

Introduction

The **Belair Early Years** series has been well-loved by early years educators working with the under-fives for many years. This re-launched edition of these practical resource books offers popular, tried and tested ideas, all written by professionals working in early years education. The inspirational ideas will support educators in delivering the three characteristics of effective teaching and learning identified in the Statutory Framework for the Early Years Foundation Stage 2012: playing and exploring, active learning, and creating and thinking critically.

The guiding principles at the heart of the EYFS Framework 2012 emphasise the importance of the unique child, the impact of positive relationships and enabling environments on children's learning and development, and that children develop and learn in different ways and at different rates. The 'hands on' activities in **Belair Early Years** fit this ethos perfectly and are ideal for developing the EYFS prime areas of learning (Communication and language, Physical development, Personal, social and emotional development) and specific areas of learning (Literacy, Mathematics, Understanding the world, Expressive arts and design) which should be implemented through a mix of child-initiated and adult-led activities. Purposeful play is vital for children's development, whether leading their own play or participating in play guided by adults. Where appropriate, suggestions for Free Play opportunities are identified.

Throughout this book full-colour photography is used to offer inspiration for presenting and developing children's individual work with creative display ideas for each theme. Display is highly beneficial as a stimulus for further exploration, as well as providing a visual communication of ideas and a creative record of children's learning journeys. In addition to descriptions of the activities, each theme in this book provides clear Learning Intentions and extension ideas and activities as Home Links to involve parents/carers in their child's learning.

This title, **I.C.T.**, particularly supports children's progress towards attaining the Early Learning Goals in the Communication and language, Understanding the world and Expressive arts and design areas of learning. The world of technology is fast-paced and, inevitably, is always evolving so that the latest innovation quickly becomes out of date. With rapid changes in the hardware and software available, even very young children are likely to be familiar with new developments such as tablet computers, smart phones, game consoles, and so on through use at home. However, the principles of encouraging children's early experiences with I.C.T. remain the same whatever hardware or software practitioners are working with. All children love working with technology and this book intends to foster a creative and playful interaction with I.C.T. The book contains many innovative and creative ideas for children to:

- Develop natural curiosity and creativity through playful I.C.T. activities.
- Develop communication and literacy skills.
- Express their thoughts and ideas through technology.
- Collaborate with other children in a fun and stimulating environment.
- Bridge the gap between technology at home and school with imaginative home activities.

I hope that adults and children alike will enjoy exploring the activities in this book.

Graham Parton

Creating a Computer Area

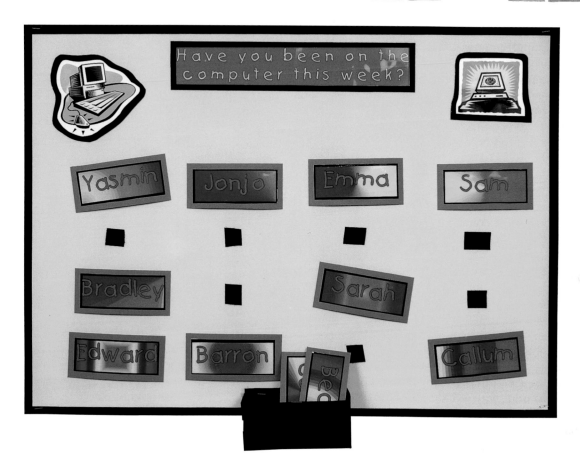

- Make the computer area as interesting as possible by adding bright backing paper and colourful images to display boards (see photograph on pages 6–7).

- Give the area a fun and stimulating theme and title, such as 'Computer Games' or 'Dinosaurs on the internet' and display the children's work associated with these themes. Try to change the theme regularly to encourage the children to visit the area.

- Create a covered board with fabric-fastenings and entitle it 'Have you been on the computer today?'. Make some cards with the children's names on and attach a fabric fastening to the back of each. These can be used to check who has been on the computer and, more importantly, who has not!

- Encourage the children to cut out pictures of computer hardware, such as monitors, keyboards, mice and speakers from catalogues and magazines. Label and display the pictures in the computer area.

- Find pictures of other items linked to ICT, such as DVD players, electronic toys, mobile phones and remote control toys, and add these to the display.

- Create specific places for items within the computer area. For example, put the roamers in their own area so that the children can easily find them and put them back.

- Place CD-Roms together in boxes, or stack them neatly, so that the children can choose their own CD-Roms and also keep them tidy. They can be sorted into themes, such as Literacy or Mathematics.

- Put printer paper into a tray so that the children can feed paper in themselves. Sort the paper into different colours and sizes.

- Ask the children where they have seen computers. Discuss what we use a computer for. Ask the children to draw pictures showing these uses and display them in the computer area with labels.

- Add computer-generated labels identifying the different parts of the computer, such as the monitor, mouse and keyboard. Make the labels big and bold to enable the children to recognise these words quickly and to begin to use the terminology.

- Place plenty of questions on cards in the computer area. For example: 'Do you have a computer at home?' 'Can you turn a computer on?' 'Can you write your name?' Make the questions as visual as possible so that the children can decode the words. Read the questions out to the children.

- Highlight a specific piece of software that the children will be using. Display cards which show the children how to use the software, for example 'How to print your work' or 'How to save your work'. Ask the children to design their own cards to help other children use the software.

Safety Points

- Make sure the computer area is a safe place to be. Tidy and sort all loose cables so that children cannot trip over them.

- Always check the equipment within the computer area for safety. Check for loose connections into the computer. Do this activity with the children to show which cables go into the computer. With your help, ask them to fit the cables into the back of the computer.

- Supply the computer area with some comfortable chairs that are the correct size for the table. Try to encourage the children to sit up when using the computer and not to stare at the screen for too long. They should not look at a screen for more than fifteen minutes at a time. A filter for the computer screen is a very good idea as this reduces most of the glare and allows children to use the computer for longer periods.

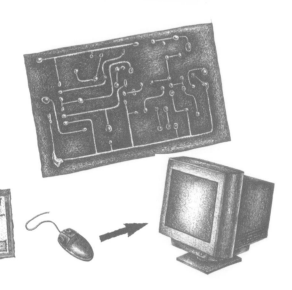

Using a Computer Suite

- The thought of taking a class of younger children into a computer suite can be a frightening experience for both the teacher and the children, but careful preparation can make the experience rewarding.

- Make sure you have at least one assistant to help the children with any problems. The more adult involvement, the better.

- Let the children visit the computer room before doing any activities. Point out where everything is and let them sit by a computer. Show them how to log-on and log-off. The children should have a username and password to log on to the network.

  ⚠ **Note:** Go through the rules of the room so that they are aware of the safety issues. Ask them why they shouldn't run in the computer room.

- Have a good look at the software on the computers and evaluate their relevance to young children – but, remember to be imaginative!

- Let the children select a program to use or load it for them beforehand. It is useful to begin with a piece of software such as a graphics program that they are familiar with or a CD-Rom that they have used before. This will give them confidence in making the transition from their computer in class to the computer suite.

- Try to design activities that encourage the children to collaborate in groups. For example, ask a group of children to colour in a template in a graphics program, using the 'paint' and 'fill' buttons.

- Above all, let the children have fun on the computers but manage the time effectively so that you can help individual children with problems.

Creating a Role-play Area

Starting Points

● Discuss the importance and use of technology in everyday life. What sorts of technology do the children use at home? Do they use the telephone? Can they change the channel on the television? How do they do this? How do they listen to music at home? Can they change the compact disc in a CD player?

● Make sure the children can record using a recording device. Use a device with large buttons and glue labels such as 'play', 'record' and 'fast forward' onto or near the relevant buttons.

Office Role-play Area

Include the following items:

- telephone and/or mobile telephone (real or toy)
- fax machine (if you cannot get hold of one of these, ask the children to make one from cereal packets, etc.)
- computer
- answering machine
- trays containing different-sized and coloured paper, envelopes, labels and stamps
- pots of pens and pencils
- telephone directories.

● Display questions in the role-play area to make the children think about the technology they are using. For example: 'Can you write a letter to your friend on the typewriter?' 'Can you use the fax machine?' 'What does the answering machine do?'

Home Role-play Area

Include the following items:

- television
- recording device
- portable music device or dictating machine
- radio (clock radio or radio tape recorder)
- CD player
- telephone and answering machine
- paper for letter-writing, pens, envelopes and stamps.

A real television and recording device could be included for the children to watch in the role-play area.

● Discuss with the children the equipment needed in the role-play area. Ask them what pieces of technology they have at home.

● While the children are role-playing in the area, ask how they use the technology: 'What do you press to phone someone?' 'What noise does the phone make when you receive a call?' 'Can you make the radio work?' 'What happens when you move the tuning dial?'

Additional Themes

● Various role-play areas can be created incorporating different technology. For example:

- a library with a computer in it to record which books have been taken out and brought back

- a surgery with computers, electronic heart and blood-pressure kits, X-rays and general equipment used by a doctor. Alternatively, set up a vet's surgery or a hospital area.

Introducing the Computer

Learning Intentions

- To become familiar with hardware and software.

- To gain basic skills, allowing children to use the computer independently.

- To become familiar with the keyboard and be able to use a mouse successfully.

- To become familiar with concept keyboards and roamers.

Starting Points

- Take a group of children into the new computer area and introduce them to the pieces of hardware. Show them the different items, such as the printer. Open the printer up so that the children can see the ink cartridges and mechanisms inside, but don't allow them to touch anything.

- Show the children the computer. Discuss how they turn the computer on, which buttons they should press and what happens when you press certain buttons.

- Look at the back of the computer and all the leads. Trace the leads to the pieces of hardware and identify each one. For example: 'This lead goes to the printer.' 'The speakers plug in here.'

- Look at the keyboard with the children. Can they identify some of the letters? Can they find the letter that starts their name? Place large, colourful lower-case stickers on the keys to make them easier to recognise.

● Look at some of the basic software packages that the children will use. Show them how to start the program from the desktop, put paper in the printer and print out their results using a specific button. Also show the children how to exit from the program. This will give them the necessary skills to use the computer by themselves.

● Show the children how to save their work and record their achievements by printing and filing. Produce individual folders for the children's work. Print out a title for the front cover, for example 'Rajid's Computer Book' and add a computer-generated illustration or a photograph of the child.

● Split the children into 'colour' groups and encourage each group to work on a different coloured USB stick.

● To make the sticks easier to identify, you could ask the children to draw a favourite picture or write their names onto sticky labels fixed to the USB sticks.

Developing Mouse Skills

- This should be one of the first skills the children develop as it is needed to work most programs. There is a wide variety of mice to choose from, although trackball mice are good for small hands as they have a ball on top which the children can use to manipulate the cursor around the screen.

- Use software for developing young children's mouse skills. Any piece of software that requires the children to use the mouse to catch things on the screen and to click on pictures will help them to gain confidence in using a mouse.

- Use a graphics manipulation software that allows a character, such as a teddy, to be dressed. Ask the children to pick the items of clothes up and move them around the screen. Talk to the children about what they are doing and allow them plenty of time to practise.

- Ask the children to place each item where they think it should go and to drop it by clicking the mouse button. Ask them how they did this. Did they put it in the right place?

- Encourage the children to use their whole hand to move the mouse and their finger to click the button without lifting their hand. Many children will place the mouse where they want it, take their hand away and then click the button – a technique which can lead to inaccuracies and a loss of confidence.

- Play computer games that require using the mouse as a bat, such as tennis or table tennis.

Concept Keyboards

- Use a concept keyboard. These are pieces of computer hardware that allow young children to input words and pictures onto the screen. Keyboard overlays can be made using a piece of software that tells the computer which word needs to appear on the screen when a certain part of the keyboard is pressed. The overlays can incorporate children's drawings which will come up with the word when pressed.

- Use a manufactured keyboard overlay. Let the children press the buttons and see the results. This will help them become familiar with concept keyboards. Allow lots of practice with such overlays before they make their own.

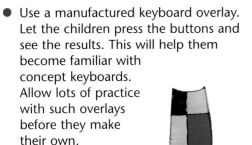

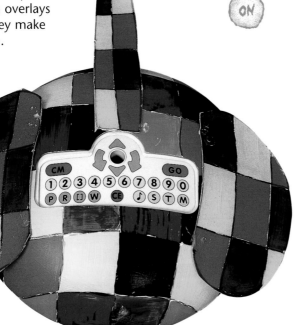

Turtles and Roamers

- Turtles and roamers seem odd to children at first. Before undertaking major activities it is important to give the children time to play with them. Ask questions such as: 'What happens when you press this button?' 'How do you make it go backwards?'

Home Links

Ask parents or carers to:

- use computers with their children at home and encourage their children to bring any examples of their work into school to show the class

- take their children to a library where computers are available and look at CD-Roms together

- take their children to a cybercafé, where they can use the internet.

Concept Keyboards in Literacy

Learning Intentions

- To gain alphabetic and phonic knowledge through sounding and naming each letter of the alphabet (using lower- and upper-case letters).

- To link sound and spelling patterns by using knowledge of rhyme to identify families of rhyming words.

- To expect written text to make sense and to check for sense if it does not.

- To recognise printed and handwritten words in a variety of settings.

Starting Points

- Use manufactured overlays that come with some early-learning software. Experiment with the large keys and the directional keys.

- Ask the children to draw an item that has the same initial letter as in their name, for example a gorilla for 'Graham'. Put the picture of the gorilla onto an overlay and use a software program that will put the word 'Gorilla' onto the screen when the picture is pressed.

Activities

- Ask the children to draw a picture for each letter of the alphabet. Incorporate these onto an overlay. Then use a software program to put the correct letter onto the screen when the picture is pressed.

- Ask the children to choose a picture that begins with a particular letter. The children then press the picture that begins with that letter. The letter will come up on the screen to reinforce the child's choice.

- Create an overlay that incorporates words at the top and an alphabetic keyboard at the bottom. Ask the children to spell the words using the letters below. They can press the word first or afterwards to discover the correct spelling.

- Create an overlay with starting words on the right-hand side, for example 'the', 'big', 'boy', 'girl', and the same words on the left-hand side, but mixed up. Ask the children to match the words by pressing them on both sides.

- Use a multimedia word processor to design your own screens.

- Scan some pictures from a book and place them in the wrong order onto the screen. The children must use the mouse to move the pictures into the correct order.

- Insert some words onto the screen and then place the letters that make up the words at the top in the wrong order. The children must drag the letters to the words.

- Create an overlay of onsets and rimes, for example 'cat', 'bat', 'sat'. Include the onset 'c', 'b', 's' and then the rime, for example 'at'. Link the overlay to the computer, so that when children press the concept keyboard, the letters will appear on the screen. Go on to incorporate two rimes, such as 'at' and 'an'. Record the words they have created by saving them into their own files.

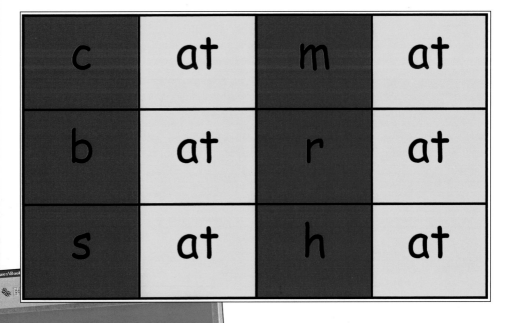

- Set up a multimedia word processor so that when the child presses the onset and rime, the program will say it, for example 'c', then 'at', and then 'cat'.

- Place pictures and words that match each other on the screen. Encourage the children to drag the matching picture to the word.

- Create a screen with the letters of the alphabet on the top half and also on the bottom half, but with all of them out of order. Ask the children to drag a letter from the top half to the corresponding letter in the bottom half. If you use two colours, the dragged letter can be moved to sit on top of the corresponding letter.

- Next, using the same screen, replace the bottom half with upper-case letters and ask the children to match the upper-case letters with the lower-case letters.

- Type in some high frequency words (such as 'dog', 'go', 'went' and 'you') on the screen. Ask the children to match them by dragging a word to its matching pair.

- Place letters on the screen that can be made into consonant-vowel-consonant (cvc) words and ask the children to make up as many different words as possible.

- Place families of rhyming cvc words and ask the children to match them up, saying the words aloud as they drag them together. Two examples of rhyming families are: 'cat', 'fat', 'mat' and 'hop', 'top, 'mop'.

- To extend the use of a simple multimedia word processor, let the children use a normal keyboard to input text onto the screen. Start by asking them to use the keyboard to type their name.

- It is important to let the children have freedom to experiment with a multimedia word processor. Ask them to spell the words phonetically first, and then get the computer to say the word to see if it is the same. In this way, the children can write many things without having to use a concept keyboard. Themes for their writing could include: 'My favourite food', 'My favourite toys'.

- Don't use the spell checker straight away. Let the children use emergent writing at first to give them confidence in using the word processor. Once they have finished their piece of work get the computer to say the whole sentence. This can then be used to check the writing at a phonetic level.

- Once the children have finished their writing, let them play with the size of the writing, the colour and where it is positioned on the screen.

- Ask the children to choose some clipart or to scan pictures from a favourite book. Place the pictures on the page and encourage the children to label them using a keyboard.

- Ask the children to print their work out and put it in their folder as a record of achievement.

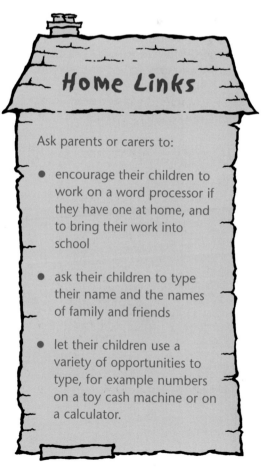

Home Links

Ask parents or carers to:

- encourage their children to work on a word processor if they have one at home, and to bring their work into school

- ask their children to type their name and the names of family and friends

- let their children use a variety of opportunities to type, for example numbers on a toy cash machine or on a calculator.

Talking Books

Learning Intentions

- To recognise printed and handwritten words in a variety of settings.

- To understand and correctly use terms about books and print, for example: book, cover, title, beginning, end, page, line, word, letter.

Starting Points

- It is important to make the transition from 'real' books to talking books as smooth as possible. Allow very young children to become familiar with the organisation of real books first so they know, for example, that the pictures carry meaning and that a book has a beginning and an end.

- Discuss with the children what makes a story. Why do stories have pictures? Why do we have words and pictures together? Which are the children's favourite books?

- Encourage the children to make up some stories on familiar themes. Working in groups, discuss what elements they want in the story, and which bits of the story each child would like to illustrate and write. Each child can complete one page.

- Create a concept keyboard with words and pictures associated with a book the children are writing themselves. The words that the children want can then be printed out and put alongside the pictures they have painted either on a computer graphics program or on paper with paints.

- Demonstrate how the children will use the computer. Show flashcards of the items they will use to navigate the talking book, such as the buttons to press to go back.

- Place the computer in the reading corner so that the talking books are in the same environment as the 'real' books. Remember to use headphones to keep the area quiet.

Activities

- Ask the children to press characters on the screen to see what they say or do.

- Encourage them to click on words that they think they know to check they are correct. Can they guess the meaning of words that they think they don't know before pressing?

- Ask the children to predict what will happen next in the story.

- Help the children to match the words with the pictures. Ask questions such as: 'Where is the owl?' 'Can you find the word for owl?' Try to use high-frequency words in your questions.

- Using the 'real' book, ask the children to say how it is different. Which is better? Which is the easier to read?

Most mornings, the sun rose to greet the day and the mockingbird sang outside an upstairs window. Inside the tree house, Brother Bear and Sister Bear would wake up.

Hot Day - intro (Menu: F10)

A Very Hot Day

CAMBRIDGE READING

SHERSTON

Juliet Partridge
Pictures by Sami Sweeten

Hot Day - page4 (Menu: F10)

Socks on the stair.

English   Spanish

The Berenstain Bears

GET IN A FIGHT

READ TO ME   LET ME PLAY

OPTIONS   QUIT

All About Me

Learning Intentions

- To promote children's understanding of ICT, other than the use of computers.

- To understand that writing can be used for a range of purposes.

Starting Point

- A good time to introduce young children to cameras is during a visit by a school photographer. Allow the children to observe the photographer at work, pointing out the setting up of an appropriate background, the careful positioning of the subject, the use of a tripod to steady the camera, and how the umbrellas reflect the light.

Activities

- Set up a miniature photographic studio in a corner of the classroom. Create an appropriate backdrop and, if possible, include a tripod, umbrellas, spotlights, clothes for role-play and a variety of old or toy cameras.

- Talk about how to use a real camera effectively: remember to get the head and shoulders of the subject in the viewfinder; try to keep the camera still while taking the photograph; if possible use a tripod to steady the camera.

- Groups of four children can role-play a photographer and photographer's assistant, who take the photographs, and two studio assistants who arrange the setting and backdrop indoors or outside. Provide a large camera that is easy to operate or a disposable camera. Children can take turns to have their photograph taken.

- Encourage the children to write about themselves using a concept keyboard. Make a simple overlay with the appropriate words on it, for example: 'My name is ... . I am ... years old. My best friend is ... .' This can be cut and pasted onto an outline of the person. Use these to make a display entitled 'All about me'.

- Using the printed photographs, cut and paste them onto the outlines in the 'All about me' display.

- Take pictures with a digital camera. Place the picture files onto a computer-generated template. Place labels on top and then print out as a complete picture.

- Take photographs of individual children when they are in dressing up clothes and mount each photograph on a separate piece of card. Make the cards into a book by punching a hole at the top, middle and bottom of each one and tying a string through each hole. Then cut the book in three, horizontally, to make a flip book. Can the class match up correctly the top, middle and bottom of each child in the book?

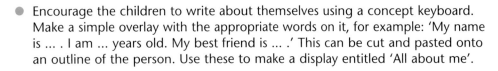

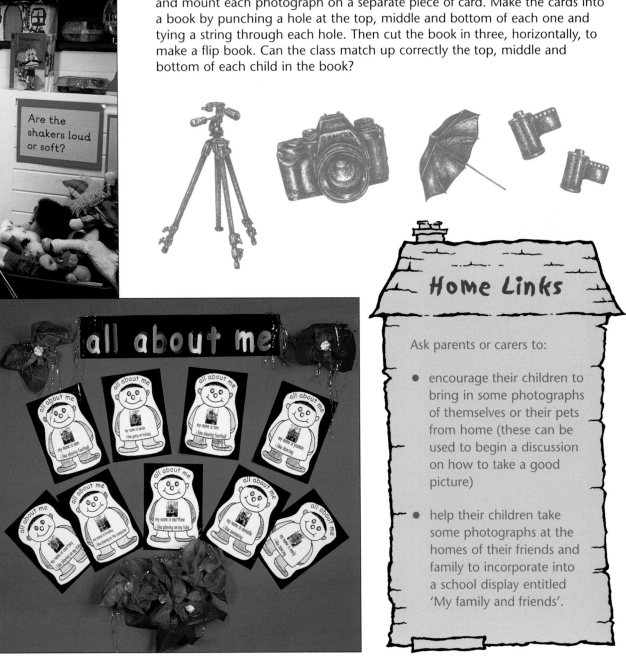

Home Links

Ask parents or carers to:

- encourage their children to bring in some photographs of themselves or their pets from home (these can be used to begin a discussion on how to take a good picture)

- help their children take some photographs at the homes of their friends and family to incorporate into a school display entitled 'My family and friends'.

Exploring Prepositions

Learning Intentions

- To explore the use of prepositions in a familiar context.

- To explore how to explain the position of an object or person.

Starting Points

- Position the computer so that everyone can see it. Discuss how to access an appropriate program. Use graphic manipulation software that allows an object, such as a teddy, to be moved alongside, inside, behind and on top of other items. The program should also reveal hidden items behind doors, etc.

we found teddy using the mouse

these are some to describe wh

behind

in front of

HONE

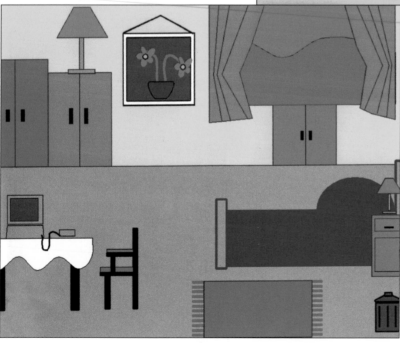

- Open the appropriate screen and ask the children: 'What can you see in this picture?' Encourage them to explain where the objects on the screen are in relation to each other, for example: 'The bed is next to the lamp.' 'The apple tree is outside the window.'

- Ask the children to hide a real object in the classroom for others to find. Once it has been found, that child tells the class where he or she found it.

- Explain to the children that Little Red Riding Hood is lost in the forest and needs to find her way to Grandma's house before the wolf eats her up. Using the roamer as the wolf, ask the children to press the 'forward' button followed by the number they think will allow the wolf to catch up with Little Red Riding Hood.

- Allow the children five attempts before saying that Little Red Riding Hood has successfully reached Grandma's house.

Different Characters

- Decorate the roamer to represent other popular story characters, such as:

  - Postman Pat: The roamer can be made to look like Postman Pat and then be programmed to find his lost cat, Jess, who is stuck up a tree.

  - The Three Little Pigs: Dress the roamer as the wolf again and also make the three little pigs with the children. The children can then program the roamer to catch the pigs or blow the pigs' houses down.

- If you have two roamers, decorate them to look like racing cars and create a start and finish line. The children then have to program the roamer to cross the finish line, using 'forward' and a number, in as many goes as they need. For example, the children might press 'forward' and then the number 3 so that the roamer goes half way down the racetrack. They can then press 'cancel', 'forward' and 3 again so that it will go past the finish line. The roamer that gets past the finish line in the least amount of turns wins the race.

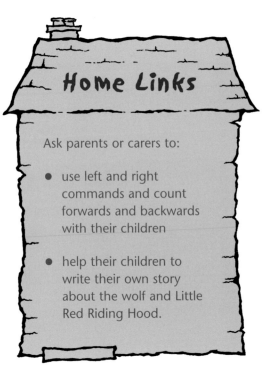

Home Links

Ask parents or carers to:

- use left and right commands and count forwards and backwards with their children

- help their children to write their own story about the wolf and Little Red Riding Hood.

Writing My Name

Learning Intentions

- To refine motor skills using computer hardware.

- To encourage an awareness of own identity and its importance.

Starting Points

- Ask the children to paint their names using different coloured paints and large pieces of paper. Encourage them to talk about the stages they went through. For example:

  – getting the brush
  – choosing the colour to paint with
  – putting the paint onto the brush
  – moving the brush on the paper to make the first letter of their name
  – selecting colours for different letters.

We have been painting our name using a program called 'Paint' We used rainbow colours to write our name

We painted our
and used clip

Activities

- Use an art software package that has lots of brush sizes and the option to incorporate stamps (pictures which the children can 'stamp' onto the page). Check that the package has functions to erase and to clear the screen totally, if necessary.

- Ask the children how they write the first letter of their name, demonstrating it by writing in the air with a finger. Help them to trace the shape using the mouse but without pressing any buttons. Let them try this until they are happy to press the button and paint the letter. Repeat for each letter of their name.

We put 'clipart' around our names and then saved our work onto a 'floppy disc'. Can you paint your name using a computer?

- If the children find a mouse too difficult, try a graphics tablet or a touch-pad.

- If the children make a mistake, they can either use the eraser if it is only one letter that has gone astray, or use the button that completely wipes the screen.

- Set the colour of the paint to 'rainbow' for multi-coloured lettering (see photographs above).

- After painting their name, decorate it with pictures from the art package. Let the children pick the image they want and stamp it onto the paper.

- Print out the decorated names. Open up the printer so the children can see the ink being laid onto the paper.

- Display the print outs along with collage self-portraits of the children. Label with details on how the names were written and decorated.

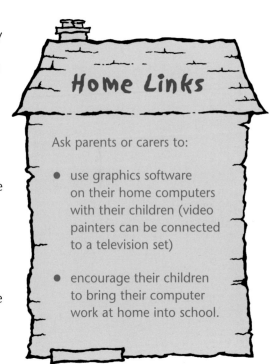

Home Links

Ask parents or carers to:

- use graphics software on their home computers with their children (video painters can be connected to a television set)

- encourage their children to bring their computer work at home into school.

Concept Keyboards in Mathematics

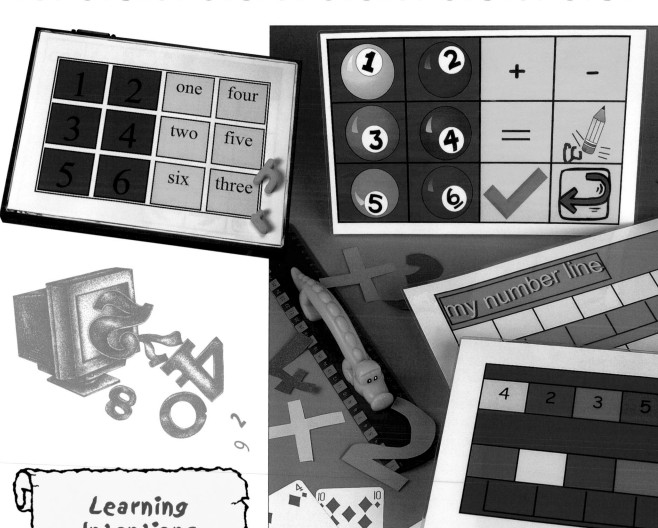

Learning Intentions

- To recognise the numerals 1 to 9.

- To use language such as 'more' or 'less', 'greater' or 'smaller', 'heavier' or 'lighter', and to compare two numbers.

- To begin to relate 'addition' to combining two groups of objects and 'subtraction' to taking away.

Starting Points

- Practise ordering cards numbered 1 to 10 and identifying them. Ask the children to collect specific numbers of objects from around the classroom, such as three colouring pens.

- Using two sets of cards numbered 1 to 10, help the children to match the numbers.

Numbers

- Create a concept keyboard that has the numerals 1 to 6 on one side and the words for the matching numbers on the other (see photograph on page 30). The children should match the number with its word.

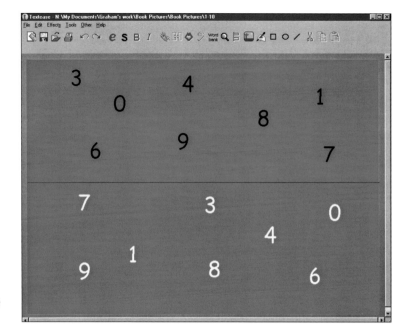

- Create an overlay that incorporates a number line from 1 to 10. Do not print the numbers on top of the number line, instead add empty white squares. Program the keyboard to output the correct number when a child presses inside the white squares. Ask the children to predict the number before they press a square. Can they work out the number by counting up the number line?

- Use a multimedia word processing program to create a screen that contains some of the numbers from 0 to 9 in the top, and repeat in the bottom half. Mix the numbers up in each half (see photograph above). The children must match the numbers by dragging the top number to the matching bottom number.

- Make a screen that contains the numerals and their matching words and ask the children to match the number with the word.

- Incorporate sets of common objects on a concept keyboard. The children must press one set and then press the picture showing one more item or one less item than in the original picture.

- Then, using the same keyboard, count how many items there are altogether in two sets and then click the appropriate set for the total.

- Make a screen that includes sets of familiar items, such as cars, animals and people. Place the numbers '1' to '5' below these and ask the children to predict the numbers in the sets by dragging each number to the correct set. They can then count the items to see if they were correct.

- Create a screen that includes a set of items, for example sweets. Ask the children to drag the sweets to make two sets. Ask: 'How many sweets are in each set?' Drag the sweets into one group again and ask the children to take one or two sweets away from the pile. Then ask: 'How many sweets are left?' Continue with similar addition and subtraction activities.

Which bottle is full, empty and half full?

| full | empty | half full |

Shape, Space and Measure

● Create a screen which includes pictures of containers that are full, half full and empty. Discuss with the children which they think is which. Add the words to the screen so the children can drag the appropriate label to each picture.

● On screen, use pictures which are either taller or shorter than one another. Sort the objects into the correct order, from tallest to shortest or vice versa.

● On screen, use pictures of small, large and middle-sized items. Sort the objects into the correct order, from smallest to biggest, or vice versa.

● Put three objects of different lengths onto a screen and then ask the children to put the items in order of length. Ask questions such as: 'Which is the longest?' 'Which is the shortest?'

● Place pictures onto the screen depicting typical times of the day, such as eating breakfast and home time. Drag the pictures into the right sequence and then print out.

● Place the days of the week onto a screen and mix them up. Children can put them into the correct order.

who is the tallest?   who is the shortest?

shortest   middle sized   tallest

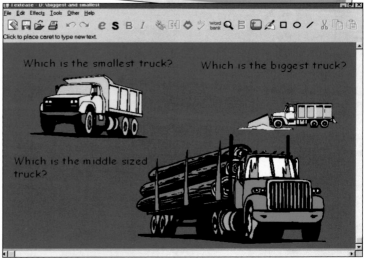

Which is the smallest truck?   Which is the biggest truck?

Which is the middle sized truck?

- Make a screen that includes pictures of people at different stages of their lives, such as a baby, infant, teenager and adult. Ask the children to sort these into the correct order. Ask questions such as 'Who do you think is the oldest?' 'Who is the youngest?', etc.

- Create a screen or concept keyboard that incorporates basic shapes and the matching words. Ask the children to either press the shape and the corresponding word or drag the word to the shape.

- Make a screen that includes a collection of basic shapes for the children to manipulate to make a pattern or picture.

- Create a screen that starts a repeating pattern and ask the children to continue the pattern by dragging shapes up from below.

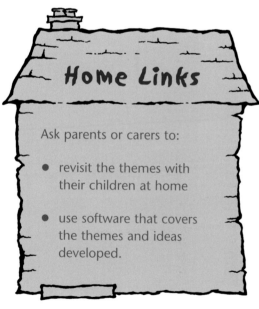

Home Links

Ask parents or carers to:

- revisit the themes with their children at home

- use software that covers the themes and ideas developed.

- Put solid shapes, such as cubes, cones and spheres, at the top of a screen and the names of these shapes at the bottom. Ask the children to drag the word to the correct shape. Use a talking word processing program to get the picture to say its shape when the child presses it.

- Put one shape in different sizes on a screen. The children can then order them in relation to their size.

- Place pictures of different denominations of money onto a screen. Suitable pictures can be found in many clipart collections or real coins can be scanned in. Encourage the children to experiment with these coins by dragging them around the screen. Coins can then be grouped according to their value.

- Place shop items with their price onto the top half of a screen and denominations of money at the bottom, making sure that each item costs only one coin value. Ask the children to drag the correct coin to the value of the item.

Getting Home

Learning Intentions

- To explore relationships between numbers.

- To understand the sequence of numbers.

Starting Points

- Decorate a roamer with painted card so that it looks like a spaceship. Design and make a model of the Earth. Tell the children that the spaceship needs to get back to Earth before its fuel runs out or it will drift in space forever!

- Revise the 'forward' command and encourage the children to estimate the number they think should be pressed to get the roamer home.

- To extend the activity, add a few obstacles so that the children have to press the 'left' and 'right' buttons on the roamer. To make this easier, the distance the roamer turns can be altered so that the children only need press '1' for each 90 degree turn. If they want it to do a full turn, they will only have to press 'right' and '4', rather than 'right' and '360'. To program the roamer to do this, press the 'right' button and then the brackets symbol, then type in '90' and the bracket button again.

- Ask questions such as: 'How many red cars did we see?' 'Which colour car did we see the most of?' 'How many more red cars were there than blue cars?'

- Transfer the results onto a spreadsheet program. Construct a graph with the coloured cars along the bottom axis. Children can transfer their results by clicking on the cars. When they do this a car of that colour is added to the graph.

- Print the results out and display the computer graphs. Alongside, place the photograph of the graph made using bricks. This will show the transition from the concrete experience of data-handling to using the computer.

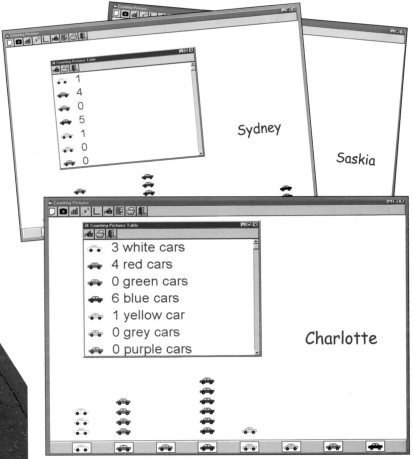

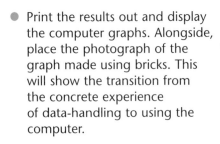

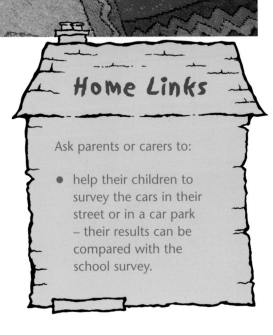

Home Links

Ask parents or carers to:

- help their children to survey the cars in their street or in a car park – their results can be compared with the school survey.

Concept Keyboards in Science and Humanities

Learning Intentions

- To describe simple features of objects, living things and events.

- To observe and describe a range of animals in terms of features such as colour and size.

- To recognise a range of animals.

- To be aware of different types of weather.

Starting Points

- Ask the children to paint or draw pictures of familiar animals.

- Look at pictures of these animals and discuss the similarities and differences between them. Discuss with the children the common characteristics of certain animals, for example, that cows and sheep have four legs but humans only have two.

Animals

- Create a concept keyboard with pictures and the names of animals. Children press the animal and then the word. Program the concept keyboard to output the word when the child presses the picture or the word.

- Mix up the words on the keyboard so that children have to search for the word after they have pressed the picture.

- Investigate what animals eat. Use a concept keyboard with pictures of animals and what they eat. Mix the food pictures and ask the children to press an animal picture and then what it likes to eat (see photograph on page 40). Program the keyboard so that, for example, when the tiger picture is pressed, 'The tiger eats' comes up on screen, and when the meat picture is pressed, 'meat' comes up.

- Look at the different stages in an insect's life, for example a butterfly. Ask the children to draw a picture for each stage. Scan them into a multimedia word processor. Mix up the pictures on a screen and ask the children to sequence them in the correct order.

Weather and Seasons

- Record the weather using a concept keyboard. Include the words 'today is' and pictures of different types of weather. Update and print out a weather report for each day.

- Add a title to the weather report keyboard, for example 'My weather forecast', or an option such as 'I like it when' for the children to record the weather they prefer.

- Use a concept keyboard with winter and summer clothes. Children can match the items they wear in each season. Include the words 'In winter I like to wear', and 'In summer I like to wear'. Program the keyboard to say the words of the clothes when pressed.

- Use a concept keyboard with pictures of different types of homes (house, bungalow, apartment). Include the words 'I live in a'.

- Create a screen that includes pictures of the same scene in each season. Add words for each season. Ask the children to match the season with the word. Program the word processor to say the word when pressed.

Home Links

Ask parents or carers to:

- encourage their children to collect pictures from magazines of familiar animals and bring them into school to make a book of animals. (These could be scanned in to make an electronic scrapbook of their favourite animals.)

Making 3D Minibeasts

Starting Points

- Take the children out to observe a variety of insects and other minibeasts, such as caterpillars, snails and spiders.

- Ask the children to draw the minibeasts. Use a magnifying glass to observe them closely. If necessary, show the children pictures of the creatures and point out the details. Paint the drawings with colours to match those observed.

- Help the children to print out labels to go with each picture.

- Display the pictures on green card. Cut the card into leaf shapes. Add a card twig and display with model insects and dried leaves, if available.

- Make an insect or spider out of reclaimed materials.

Activities

- Use a graphics program to draw pictures of insects. Make sure the children pay close attention to the features of their minibeast. Allow the children plenty of time to practise – mistakes are easy to erase.

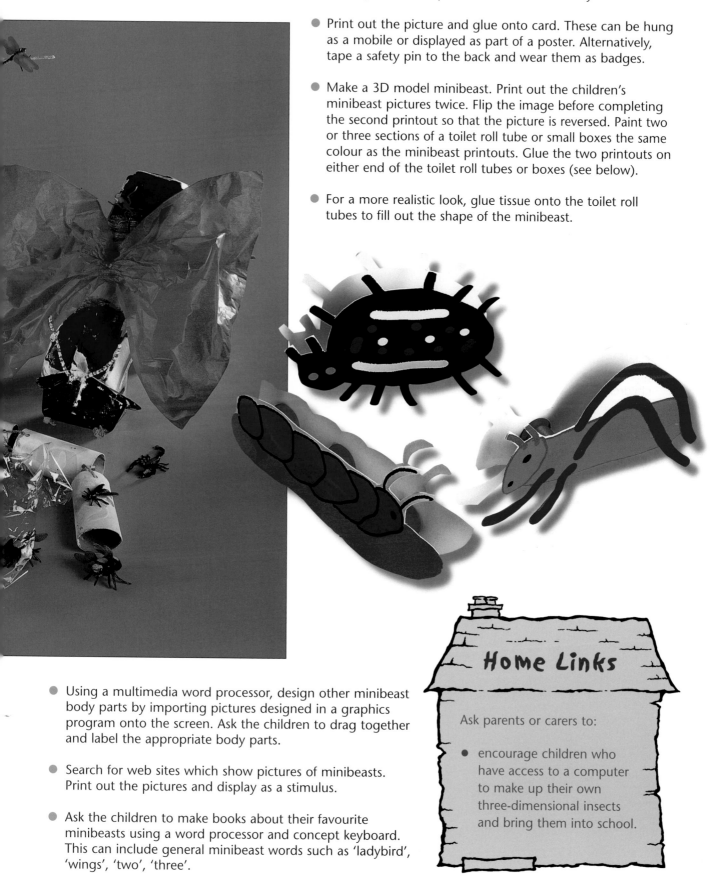

- Print out the picture and glue onto card. These can be hung as a mobile or displayed as part of a poster. Alternatively, tape a safety pin to the back and wear them as badges.

- Make a 3D model minibeast. Print out the children's minibeast pictures twice. Flip the image before completing the second printout so that the picture is reversed. Paint two or three sections of a toilet roll tube or small boxes the same colour as the minibeast printouts. Glue the two printouts on either end of the toilet roll tubes or boxes (see below).

- For a more realistic look, glue tissue onto the toilet roll tubes to fill out the shape of the minibeast.

- Using a multimedia word processor, design other minibeast body parts by importing pictures designed in a graphics program onto the screen. Ask the children to drag together and label the appropriate body parts.

- Search for web sites which show pictures of minibeasts. Print out the pictures and display as a stimulus.

- Ask the children to make books about their favourite minibeasts using a word processor and concept keyboard. This can include general minibeast words such as 'ladybird', 'wings', 'two', 'three'.

Home Links

Ask parents or carers to:

- encourage children who have access to a computer to make up their own three-dimensional insects and bring them into school.

How Do We Grow?

Learning Intentions

- To explore how humans grow.

- To develop the use of simple spreadsheet programs to look for patterns in data.

Starting Points

- Ask the children to bring in photographs of themselves as babies. Discuss with the children how they have grown since then.

- Ask questions such as: 'Do you think you grow quickly or slowly?' 'Can you see yourself growing?' 'Do you keep a chart at home to show how much you have grown?'

These are our heights

Who is the shortest?

Activities

- Give pairs of children a strip of coloured paper that is taller than them. Attach the paper strip vertically to a wall, with the bottom touching the ground. One child in a pair stands against it. The other makes a mark where the top of the child's head meets the paper. Cut the paper strip to the correct length.

- Once all the children's heights have been measured, make a graph to compare the heights of the children.

44

- Use wooden blocks as non-standard units. Count how many blocks it takes to cover the strips of paper. Transfer the information onto the computer using a simple spreadsheet program that lets the children click on a picture to count up the height of themselves in wooden blocks.

- Once all the children have contributed to the graph, print it out and display it with the other graph.

- Evaluate the way both graphs were created. Which is the easiest to get information from? Who is tallest, shortest? Who is middle-sized?

- Ask the children to line up according to their size. Encourage the children to order themselves to begin with. Ask questions such as: 'Who goes first – the shortest or the tallest?'

- Once all the children's heights have been measured with the paper strips, assemble the strips to make a bar graph. The children can then decorate the paper strips with their own designs.

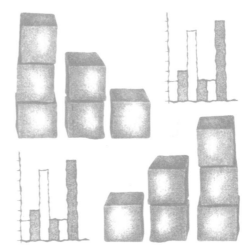

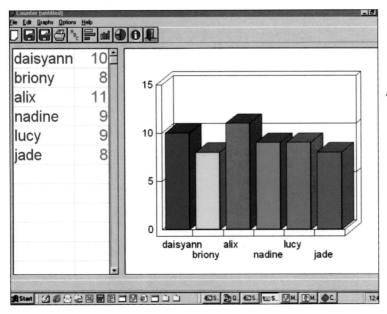

Home Links

Ask parents or carers to:

- encourage their children to keep a record of their growth using a height chart

- help their children to add the information to a spreadsheet.

Using the Internet

Learning Intentions

- To begin to utilise and enjoy the internet.

- To gain retrieval skills.

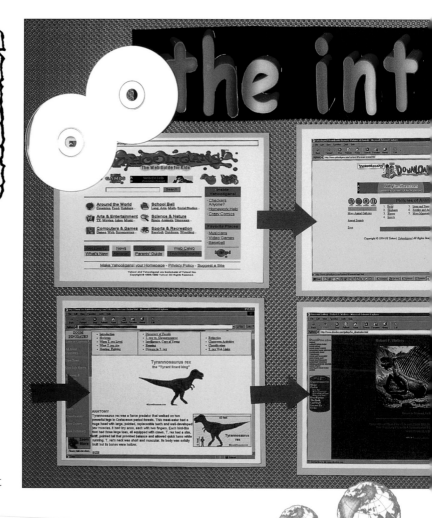

Starting Points

- Using non-fiction books, pick a topic for the children to find out about, such as dinosaurs, minibeasts, cars or houses.

- Encourage curiosity about the topic by asking guided questions. For example: 'What did dinosaurs eat?' 'Can you name the minibeasts you can find in the book?' 'Which cars do you like the best?'

- If available, introduce a television text service to the children. Let them explore it before introducing the internet.

Activities

- Children will need guidance throughout activities on the internet as it is easy for them to get lost.

- When successfully connected to the internet, explain to the children that the internet is like a telephone line that lets pictures and writing come down it. This will give the children a way into understanding what the internet is.

- Using a child-friendly search engine, put a word into the window to search for specific web sites or click a choice of categories. These categories divide into other categories and then specific web pages can be found.

- Print out pages from each stage in their search, and display.

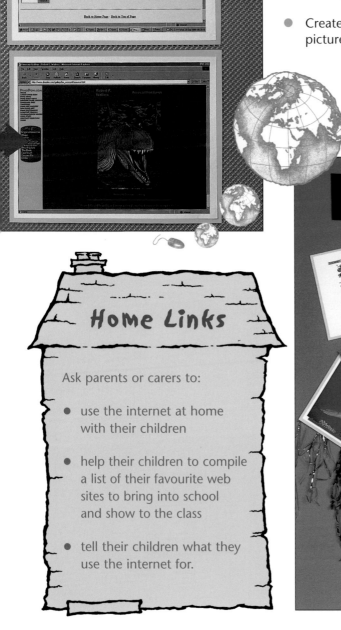

- Guide the children through the pages they find and help them with some of the main text on the page. It is very easy for the children to lose their way on the internet.

- Look for pictures on a chosen topic. For example, ask the children to search for different pictures of dinosaurs. Use the pictures to help the children describe the dinosaurs. Ask questions such as: 'Did they have sharp teeth?' 'How big do you think they were?'

- Click on items so that sounds can be heard. Remember to use headphones so that other children are not disturbed.

- Help the children to copy pictures from the internet into a word processing package.

- Create posters about dinosaurs or other subjects using pictures copied from the internet.

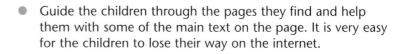

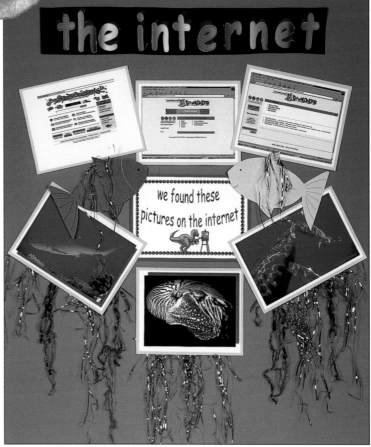

Home Links

Ask parents or carers to:

- use the internet at home with their children

- help their children to compile a list of their favourite web sites to bring into school and show to the class

- tell their children what they use the internet for.

Recording Sounds

Starting Points

● Demonstrate the use of a recording device to the children. Use a recording device with large buttons and pictorial cues for their functions.

● Let the children record themselves talking. Give them the opportunity to play with the equipment and discover the buttons' functions. Play back the recordings to the rest of the class.

● Ask the children questions such as: 'Does your voice sound the same on tape?' 'Why is it different?' 'Can you identify this voice?' 'Who can it be?' 'What did you do to record your voice?' 'Which buttons did you press?' 'Would you be able to do it again?'

Activities

● Encourage the children to go round the room, or school, and record anything they wish. Play their recordings back for the other children to guess what has been recorded.

- Play games using recordings of sounds from around the classroom or home. The children can then draw pictures to explain the sound. These can be put onto a lotto board and the children can identify the sounds with the pictures.

- Use a recording device on a 'senses walk'. If possible, use a small dictating machine which is easy to carry. Before the walk, ask the children to discuss what sounds they might expect to hear. Will they hear an elephant, or a tiger? Encourage them to visualise their walk and the sounds they expect to hear by drawing them on a flip chart.

- Once outside, encourage the children to pursue the sounds they discussed. Ask them where they might find a bird singing, or water splashing. Once they have found a sound they would like to record, give them plenty of time to get a good recording. Leave space between each recording.

- Encourage the use of the rewind button to listen to a recording to check it is good enough. If it is not, let the children try again.

- Play the recording to a group of children for them to guess what the sounds are. Discuss and explain the steps they went through to get the recordings.

- Paint pictures to explain the sounds they heard on their 'sense walk' and the process they went through to record the sounds.

Home Links

Ask parents or carers to:

- let their children interview them and take their recordings into school for the rest of the class to hear

- record sounds in the home with their children.

Exploring CD-Roms

Learning Intentions

- To extract useful information from text and pictures contained on a CD-Rom.

Starting Points

- Show the children a CD-Rom and ask them to describe it. What shape is it? What colours can they see when it is gently waved? Discuss what CD-Roms are used for.

- Show the children how to put the CD-Rom into the computer. Ask: 'What happens to the screen when you put it in?' 'Which button do you have to press to start the program?'

- Show the children some of the pages within the CD-Rom. What do they think of them? What do the pictures tell them? Can they guess the title by looking at the pictures?

Activities

- Try a CD-Rom about the human body in which the children can click on any part of the body to gain information through the pictures and animations.

Activities

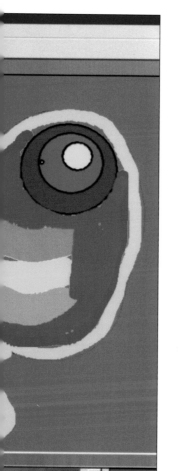

- Using a symmetry tool in a graphics program, draw an outline of a butterfly.

  - Drop shapes provided by the program, such as circles, on to one side of the outline. A corresponding shape will also appear on the other side. For variety, ask the children to try different-sized shapes.

  - When happy with their butterfly designs, the children can fill in the circles with any colours they wish, but they must make sure that they fill the corresponding shape with the same colour. Complete by filling in the surrounding outline with the colour of their choice.

  - Print out the butterfly twice and stick back-to-back on a piece of card for hanging. Hang several from the ceiling as mobiles.

  - Attach a piece of string onto the outer edge of the butterfly wings, and then another piece of string onto the bottom side of the abdomen. Hang the butterfly up by the two strings on the wings and let the third string dangle below. When you pull this the butterfly will flap its wings!

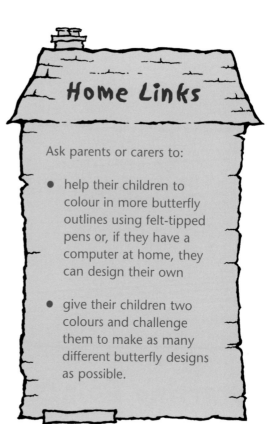

Home Links

Ask parents or carers to:

- help their children to colour in more butterfly outlines using felt-tipped pens or, if they have a computer at home, they can design their own

- give their children two colours and challenge them to make as many different butterfly designs as possible.

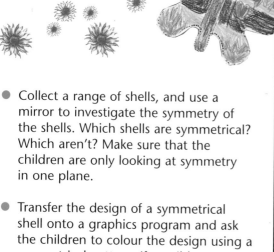

- Collect a range of shells, and use a mirror to investigate the symmetry of the shells. Which shells are symmetrical? Which aren't? Make sure that the children are only looking at symmetry in one plane.

- Transfer the design of a symmetrical shell onto a graphics program and ask the children to colour the design using a symmetrical pattern. If possible, use a program that allows you to divide the screen into a vertical plane of symmetry, so that when the children add a colour in one half it will magically appear in the other half, too.

Animal Magic

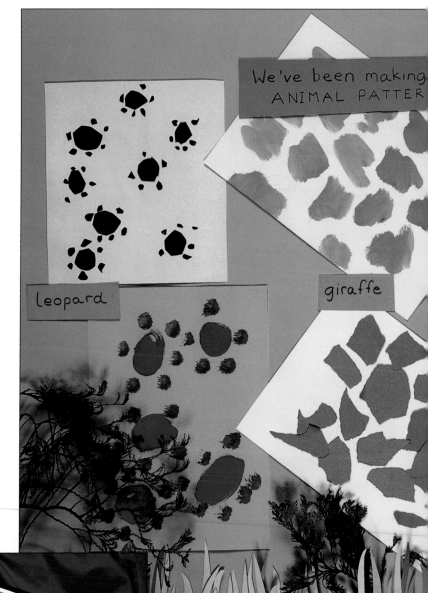

Learning Intentions

- To experience different approaches to art.

- To use fine motor skills to reproduce a picture on a computer.

Starting Points

- Go on a visit to a farm or zoo, or play a tape or video that shows various animals (wild or domesticated).

- Discuss the different animals the children saw. Ask which were their favourites, which were similar and which were different from each other.

- Ask the children to draw or paint a picture of their favourite animal using a pen and paper. Let them have lots of attempts until they are happy with the result.

We've been making ANIMAL PATTER

leopard

giraffe

Activities

- Look at the markings on animals. Repeat the patterns using paints or by cutting out shapes from coloured card and gluing them onto a coloured backing. Display against a savannah-style background with ferns and coloured paper cut into grass shapes.

Elmer

a lizard

a sheep

three tigers

- Ask the children to copy the drawing of their favourite animal on screen using a graphics program. Encourage them to explore the properties of the various sizes and shapes of brushes. Also experiment with the spray-cans and other special effects.

- Print the completed animal picture. While it is printing, open the hood of the printer so that the children can see their picture gradually appear.

⚠ **Note:** Don't let the children put their fingers into the printer or get too close in case their hair or clothing gets caught.

- Once the designs have been printed, the children can then incorporate these into various activities.

- Draw a circle around the picture and cut it out. Glue it onto a circular piece of card and cover the picture with sticky-backed plastic. Add clothes-fastening tape so that it can be worn as a very large badge (see photograph below).

- The pictures can be cut out and put onto a large piece of paper. Create text with a word processor and incorporate this onto the paper to make a poster advertising a party with an animal theme.

- Use the printed animal pictures for a display on the children's favourite animals.

- Print out children's animal designs on special iron-on printer paper and then iron this onto a white T-shirt.

- Use an LCD projector and an interactive white board, so that the children can work in a larger area. They can use their fingers to draw onto the white board.

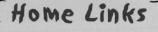

tiger

Home Links

Ask parents or carers to:

- help their children draw animals on a computer at home using drawing software

- encourage their children to explore other media too, such as collage, paint, pencils.

Gemma   Alex

Roamer Patterns

Starting Points

- Ask the children to pretend their hand is the roamer. With a pen in their hand, they should let their hand 'roam' on a large piece of paper.

- Mark arrows for 'forward', 'backward', 'left' and 'right' on flash cards. Working in pairs, one child picks a card and says a number between 1 and 10. The second child has to put their pen down onto the paper and draw in the direction on the card for as long as they think necessary to fit the number.

- Ask the children to bring in remote-control toys from home. Ask them to show the class what it can do and how they do it. In which direction is the toy going? How do they make it turn?

- Paint the tyres of a remote-control car and place it on a large piece of paper on the floor. Let the children move the car around the paper and see what sort of patterns they can get the car to make. Can it make a straight line? A circle? Can it make letters and numbers?

Activities

- Attach a pen to a roamer and program it to construct patterns using 'forward', 'back' and 'around'. Encourage the children to create all kinds of patterns and to try different-coloured pens.

- Once the children have had a chance to explore, ask them: 'What shapes can you program the roamer to make?' 'Can you make it create a square, circle or rectangle?' Encourage them to press a 'left' or 'right' button and then any number so that they discover the higher the number the further it moves.

- Extend the above activity by using a *Logo* program, and then using a concept keyboard attached to it. The children can use this to make their own patterns on the screen. On the left side of the concept keyboard, put the standard commands used for 'forward', 'right', 'left', 'backward'. On the right put 1 to 9. (See photograph on page 62.)

- Brainstorm with the children for ideas on what to draw. An idea, such as a house, can then be taken back to the pen and paper stage or the roamer stage, or it can be tried out on a concept keyboard and *Logo* program.

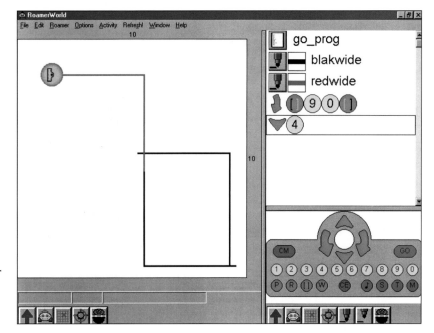

- If using *Logo,* show the commands 'penup' and 'pendown' to the children. This will give the children the ability to move around the screen without leaving a trail, so more complicated pictures can be drawn.

- If available, use *Logo* programs that replicate the command buttons on the roamer. This type of program helps the children progress from the roamer to using a *Logo* program.

- Make some flashcards with some of the more basic commands such as 'forwards', 'backwards' and play a game on the carpet. Ask one child to be the pen and other children to give the 'pen' instructions such as 'forward 5', 'backwards 5' and 'right 1'. This will give the children confidence and help them with the recognition of the words.

- Ask the children to experiment with moving the turtle around the screen. Encourage them to try to solve any problems. Ask questions such as: 'Can you make the turtle go back 1 step?' 'How do you make it turn?' To make the activity easier, program the turtle to turn in increments rather than units of degrees.

- Place some obstacles onto a *Logo* screen and ask the children to navigate the turtle around them. Incorporate a start and finish. Remember to make a 90 degree turn into one unit, so that when the children press 'left 1', the turtle will turn 90 degrees.

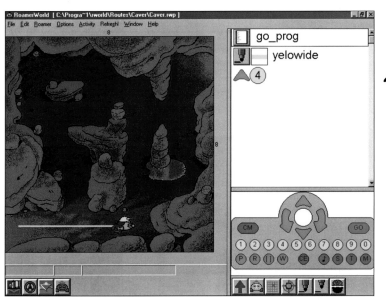

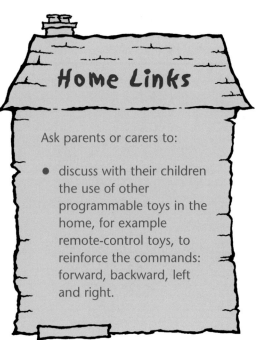

Home Links

Ask parents or carers to:

- discuss with their children the use of other programmable toys in the home, for example remote-control toys, to reinforce the commands: forward, backward, left and right.

Useful Information

Software

- The software used in this book is listed below and is available from leading educational software suppliers:

    – *Textease* by Softease Ltd

    – *My World for Windows* by Semerc Software Ltd

    – *Superlogo* by Longman Logotron Ltd

    – *Dazzle* by Silica Software

CD-Roms

- *My First Amazing World Explorer* – Dorling Kindersley

- *My First Amazing Dictionary* – Dorling Kindersley

- *Amazing Animals* – Dorling Kindersley

- *The Jolly Postman* – Dorling Kindersley

- *Cambridge Talking Books* – Sherston Software

- *Living Books* – Broderbund Software

Web Pages

- www.yahooligans.com

- www.dinodon.com/gallery